FUNDAMENTALS OF CREATIVE WRITING

Building the Foundations of a Real World

Joy A. Burke

Story Consultant & Developmental Editor

Fundamentals of Creative Writing
Building the Foundations of a Real World

www.hahaink.com

ISBN-13: 978-1511641111

Cover design by Joy A. Burke.
Photo from Pixaby.com under CC License CC0 1.0 Universal

Printed in the United States of America

Table of Contents

Fundamentals of Creative Writing

Draw your readers in by learning the fundamentals of creating fiction and non-fiction that hooks!

Haha! Ink! Creative Studios

Joy A. Burke
Story Consultant & Developmental Editor

Introduction

At some point in our lives, many of us have wanted to share with others, the worlds we create for ourselves. Whether those worlds be fictitious or memoir, you need to capture your reader and pull them in so they simply can't put the book down.

This book is an overview 'workshop' and will touch on a few of the most important elements of what creates a strong piece of fiction – or creative non-fiction.

I invite you to go through each exercise and apply it to your own writing, and continue your exploration of each topic by researching online, searching out a local class, or continuing to work with me through a tailored program. No matter what you do, you will be rewarded as you dig deeper into writing and hone your skills.

Now, on to the good stuff!

Believable Dialogue

You know you've written great dialogue when your readers don't realize they're reading it. We've all been there: so consumed by a story, that we see and hear the character talking rather than see that they're lines on a page. That is how dialogue should be written.

So how do you do it?

There are a few steps to run your dialogue through to be sure your readers will believe your characters belong.

1. Keep your dialogue consistent with the personality of your character.
2. Emulate the key components of real conversations
3. Use dialogue tags as appropriate.
4. Have dialogue move your story forward; through action or thought.
5. Limit your use of adverbs (good for all aspects of writing).
6. Read your dialogue out loud (good for all aspects of writing).

7. Practice writing the same scene from a different characters point of view.

Keep your dialogue consistent with the personality of your character

Every character in your story is created with a different personality. One of the best ways we show personality in writing is through dialogue.

Are they kind and gentle, or rough and mean? You can show this in how they speak and treat others.

Is your character an introvert but a genius, or an extrovert who is insecure? This can be shown in how much they speak, to whom, and what they say.

What country are they from (*accent*)? What region (*dialect*)? Are they religious (*habits they might refer to/attend to*)? Educated (*words they use*)?

Tons of options, and all can be hinted at through dialogue.

With some many different types of personalities, it's important to be sure you keep your characters consistent throughout your story. As you review your book, short, excerpt, etc., it is imperative you match the correct character with the correct dialogue. If you don't know and believe in your characters, why should your reader?

Emulate the key components of real conversations

How we actually speak can be boring. Next time you think about it, listen in on a conversation and think about what that might *read* like. So, we need to take the key components of real conversation and turn them into something that moves with our stories.

Take the action pieces, the story pieces, and the pieces of conversation that serve a purpose and include those in your dialogue. If it doesn't move it doesn't belong.

It's the same idea of using 'It is' versus 'it's.' 'It is' is technically the more grammatically correct way or proper way, but 'it's' is easier to say, read, and type.

Go with what your character would say. What would *you* say? It doesn't always have to be 'proper' but it does have to be real to your character. If not, the dialogue will be forced and awkward to write and read.

Use dialogue tags as appropriate

What are dialogue tags? Things like 'he said' 'she added, then laughed' 'he whispered.' Tags note who said what with a little description on how they said it.

Be careful on what descriptive words you use as your tag. For example, you would not be able to say "'You are so funny,' she laughed" because a person can't laugh words. They'd have to say the words and laugh. Or laugh, say the words, and continuing laughing. You'd be better off with, "'You are so funny,' she said laughing." It's a technicality, and most everyone reading will know what you mean, but it's one an editor will get you on.

On this same note of tags, use them as appropriate and feel free to include names of other characters in dialogue that another character is addressing, either verbally, with thought, or with an action. You don't need to use them every time someone speaks. If you only have two speakers, your reader should be able to follow along well enough to know who is who, with the occasional tag.

When you get three or more speakers, it's better to add more tags, or more names being addressed. But again, not needed after every statement. Good rule of thumb: read your dialogue out loud to someone not related to your story and see if they can follow along. Or, have them read it.

Have dialogue move your story forward; through action or thought

Writing dialogue can be challenging. But keep in mind, the goal of dialogue in your story isn't to establish pleasantries or talk about our day like we would in person, it's to move the story forward and provide insight.

While it's perfectly normal for us to chatter away in real life, in stories, that sort of back-and-forth is distracting, can bore your reader, and rarely occurs in good writing. Your reader is unaccustomed to it and while they may not know exactly what the problem is, they'll know something is off with the dialogue.

If your characters don't have a point – if they don't have a reason they are speaking to help move the story forward – they shouldn't be speaking at all.

Here's an example:

Alice jumped for the phone on the first ring.

"Hello?"

"Hi Alice, it's Mary."

"Hi Mary. What's up?"

"Oh, nothing. Just thought I'd call and say hi. What are you up to?"

"Just the same stuff. Hanging out at home, watching TV, and waiting for Jason to call. Nothing new."

Mary laughed. "Yeah, I guess not! By the way, I actually did see Jason at the mall earlier."

"What? What was he doing there?"

"I don't know. But he was with a bunch of people I didn't know. That's why I didn't see him at first. There was also some redhead hanging all over him…"

Alice continued to listen and realized this was the real reason Mary called. How could she call Mary her best friend when she constantly toyed with her like this?

This is all something we would say in a real-life situation, however on the page it's a bit painful because the point - the action – doesn't happen until line six. Then the tension picks up and we discover the true nature of Alice and Mary's friendship.

Here's another way to approach the same scenario:

Alice stared blankly at the TV screen. Another mundane Saturday. The ringing phone brought her to life and she snatched it up on the first ring.

"Hello?"

"Alice, it's Mary! You will *never* guess who I saw at the mall yesterday."

Oh no, thought Alice. *What is she going to torture me with now?* Her thoughts immediately went to her boyfriend Jason, whose silence lately had caused her to wonder exactly where they stood.

"Okay I'll just tell you since you're thinking too much, *as usual*. Jason!"

Alice's heart plummeted. "We'll you don't have to sound happy about it, Mary."

"And there was a gorgeous red-head hanging all over him. So, where were you?"

Hopefully you find the second example more engaging and see how dialogue can not only inform, but move the story along.

Limit your use of adverbs (good for all aspects of writing)

Adverbs, as a general rule, tend to detract from the strength of your dialogue. They are good words, but writers have traditionally depended on them too much to convey the meaning they are hoping their dialogue is already doing. Adverbs are oftentimes unneeded. An action or a description could be used in its place.

Simply take a look at where you've placed an adverb to see if it is helping or hindering your dialogue and if an action or description would be better suited in its place.

Here's a quick example:

Sentence using adverb:

"Well now that's a good idea isn't it?" he said <u>sarcastically</u>.

Sentences using description in place of an adverb:

"Well now that's a good idea isn't it?" he said rolling his eyes and using his John Wayne voice.

Read your dialogue aloud (good for all aspects of writing)

I am a proponent of reading all writing aloud. It does wonders for discovering inconsistencies, odd phrases, and hiccups in pacing. It's also great for hearing where your dialogue runs a little dry or feels awkward. You really don't know what your writing sounds like unless you hear it. If you only read it, your mind easily inserts how it should sound.

Practice writing the same scene from a different characters point of view

This of course is not mandatory, but I encourage you to consider this exercise. Writing the same scene from a variety of points of view or character perspectives gives you the opportunity to determine whether or not you've selected the correct character to voice it.

It also helps you get to know your characters on a more intimate level and allows them to speak to you. Sometimes, all our characters need is the opportunity to share and they'll tell us what we need to know to move our story in the right direction.

Dialogue can be one of the most difficult things to write, but it's crucial to weaving your story together. The better you know your characters – their quirks, faults, redeeming

features, what makes them laugh, what makes them cry –
the more you can convey their personalities through their
everyday speech. And the more believable your dialogue
will be.

Dialogue Exercises

Below are exercises you can work on for each component we addressed earlier as you move forward with your writing. These simple exercises are meant to help get ideas flowing and give you an opportunity to implement ideas you may have had while reading.

Keep your dialogue consistent with the personality of your character

Does your character have an accent, or is of a particular age where they speak slightly different than other characters in your story? Many of our characters talk in a specific fashion unique to them. If not with accents or dialects, with use of certain words or with certain attitudes.

Review your characters' speech to be sure it remains consistent throughout your story. You don't want your high school educated French gypsy to sound like a PhD from Scotland by the end of the story.

If you need help keeping your characters straight, map them out on paper, or highlight them in different colors on your computer with a color key code.

Emulate the key components of real conversations

As an experiment, record yourself and a willing friend conversing normally. Take that short conversation and cut out the unnecessary pieces so you get to the meat of the conversation. Then, edit what you've kept to the voice of your character.

Use dialogue tags as appropriate

As you re-read your story, check to be sure your speakers are clear. This is most easily done if you read the story aloud, or have another person read the story.

When you check for adverbs and read the story aloud, you can also check to be sure your dialogue tags are in place. Experiment with removing, replacing, rewording, and rearranging the tags to find the best use of tags and the smoothest transitions.

Have dialogue move your story forward; through action or thought

Write a scene including a good portion of dialogue, just as it comes to your mind. Don't worry about using tags or showing action – just get the bones on the page.

Go back and rewrite the scene focusing first on how you can use action to move to story forward, then again focusing on thought.

Once both have been written, see what you can pull from all three to make your final piece of writing full of action, thought, and description to create the ideal scene.

Limit your use of adverbs (good for all aspects of writing)

Select a section of your story you've already written you'd like to work on. Once printed, go through and circle all the words ending in '-ly.' As a general rule, adverbs generally end in '-ly.' Once completed, see which of these words can either be:

- Eliminated
- Changed to an action word
- Changed to a description word

Which of the above options will make your writing stronger and covey the meaning of your dialogue best? Sometimes the adverb *is* the best option, and that's okay! But it's a good idea to review the number of adverbs you are using and if they are the words that can do the best job in that particular place.

Read your dialogue out loud (good for all aspects of writing)

In this exercise, simply read portions of your story aloud. It may be helpful to read it to someone else to have that extra pair of ears listening, but do what you are comfortable with. It is important to at least read it to yourself – I can guarantee you will hear something that you'll want to tweak.

Practice writing the same scene from a different characters point of view

This exercise gives you practice in seeing and voicing the same scene from a variety of characters' point of view. It is a great exercise to help you familiarize yourself with all your characters and prepare yourself for how they will react to future situations. Even if you don't use all the scenes you write, they are beneficial to both you, your characters, and your story as you will all evolve and grow together into a more cohesive unit.

Show don't Tell

We've all heard this before, but what does it mean?

Showing allows the reader to see in their minds eye with their own imagination, the picture you've created with words.

Telling restricts that creativity. It tells them exactly what they should envision rather than allow their minds the freedom to create the scenes small details for themselves.

Here's an example:

a) He was angry.
b) Slamming the door as hard as he could, he was sure to stomp down each and every stair. Once on the cement pavers, he kicked each yard toy in his path only stopping when the pink ball burst on a tree branch. He finally flopped on the grass and ran a sore hand through his hair. He hadn't realized he'd been clenching his fists that hard.

Can you tell which one shows and which one tells?

You get much more emotion and movement from the second example. It's moved the story forward, given us some insight, and posed some questions, without anyone saying anything. What happened to make him so upset? What's he going to do about it? How will he going to go back into that house and face whatever demons he needs to face?

Showing, as you can see from our short example above, provides the reader the opportunity to create the world alongside with you, the writer; to become a part of your story and get involved with your characters. Telling, puts up an unintentional barrier between your characters and reader, and the chance for the reader to become emotionally involved has the potential to disappear.

Here's another quick and less dramatic example:

a) How could I say no when he looked at me with those bright eyes and playful smile?
b) How could I say no when he looked at me with those clear blue eyes and boyish grin?

Both are descriptive, but the first example shows, the second tells.

Re-read the examples and see what impressions you get when you try to visualize the character.

The first line simply says 'bright' eyes, which could imply a different color for different readers depending on their preference or the image they've already formed for this character. The second line tells the reader his eyes are blue. No question.

The first line states the smile is playful. Again, playful is relative. We all interpret playful differently, especially when reading facial expressions. So when I read playful, I may see something very different than 'boyish' which is what the second line states. There is also 'smile' versus 'grin', which gives a different feel as well.

No matter what stage of writing, every writer struggles with 'show; don't tell.' Professional editors even have the shorthand 'SDT' to help professional writers with their showing. So it's always a work in progress. But take the time now to get in the habit of finding areas you can show and not tell, and you'll thank yourself later!

Show Don't Tell Exercises

ONE

Rewrite these sentences to a *showing* sentence, not a telling one.

1. The dinner was delicious.
2. The thunderstorm was dramatic.
3. He loves cats.

Rewrite these sentences to a *showing* paragraph, not a telling one.

1. It was a fun trip.
2. She was so sad when her best friend moved.
3. The ocean was vast.

TWO

Look through your story for any areas you (or others) feel don't *show* anything. Passages where you read it and no images come to mind. This can be body text, dialogue, areas of action where it may not be evident action is happening, sensory imagery – anywhere in your work. Rewrite these areas using what you see in your mind's eye. (Use the examples above for inspiration if needed.)

When you originally wrote this passage, what were you thinking? What did you see? What did you feel? Write it out. It's okay if it's wordy, you can edit non-essential words later. But for now, get it all out on paper.

If you have a scene about kids coming home to freshly baked cinnamon rolls after a first day of school, and it was inspired by your grandmothers baking – write it out. Describe what the kitchen looked like: blue and white linoleum floors which reminded you of a checkerboard cake, squeaky plastic covered chairs – yours had a small tear in the plastic which you fidgeted with but tried not to make worse; the small off-white oven with a chip in it your grandmother painted in with whiteout – made you laugh but glad she took such pride in her things; and the cinnamon rolls – smelled better than the town bakery where all the other kids stopped for snacks on the way home from school. But not you, because you knew what waited for you at grandmas…

Take all those bits and combine them into what you want your readers to see and feel in that passage. Continue this throughout your story/stories. Be sure to do a 'Save As' so you can track your progress!

Character Development

A) Character Development = The creation of characters for a story.

B) Character Development = The evolution of a character within the story's framework.

The creation of characters for a story

Creating characters is one of the most fundamental pieces to creating a story. Many may find it easy to do, but others not so much. Here are some tips to keep in mind when creating characters for your story:

1. Keep them real
2. What makes them unique? What quirks do they have?
3. Consider how others in the story will react to them

Keep Them Real

Readers will believe your character, admire your character, and fall in love with your character, if they believe your character is real. So give him/her a history, personality, passions, amusements, relationships, defects, ambitions – you get the point. Create your character to be a real person so they will leap off the page and into the hearts of your readers.

Providing a lineage and biography is unnecessary; inserting little snippets here and there is all it takes. Dropping a line about her being an orphan or being adopted is enough for the reader to make certain assumptions about the character's past and upbringing and reasons for current responses to certain situations. Hinting at an anger problem will cause your reader to wonder what will happen when a situation starts to escalate in the novel. Breadcrumbs are enough.

But keep in mind, you have created a world for your characters. Be sure your character is true to that world. If you've written a story taking place in the 1900's, your character can not be using 21st century words or slang.

What makes them unique? What quirks do they have?

We all want to be able to identify with the characters we read about. If they are perfect, they become stagnant.

However, if your character is obsessed with pens and pencils and can't resist buying them every time she enters an office supply store, we'll that's something a little quirky and memorable – and potentially money draining. If your character voices their opinion each time someone irritates them, that could cause a ton of conflict and open up a lot of doors for your novel, and close many doors to solving the problem as well.

Developing idiosyncrasies, flaws, and unique traits for your character will help them become more memorable and give readers a chance to relate to relate to them.

Consider how others in the story will react to them

The dynamics between characters is what keeps the story interesting. If you have an interesting and volatile character with no one to respond to his actions, the story is relatively dead. But if you have a cast of other characters all with their own unique personas, ready to respond in different ways to his actions, as well as each other's, you will have a variety of results which can move your story in countless directions.

So as you build each character, consider their role in the overall framework of the story. Sometimes you won't know. You may plan on them playing one role, but as the story develops, that particular character's place in it changes and they may become a more or less powerful force. Let the characters react to each other how they will and the story will become what it was meant to be.

The evolution of a character within the story's framework

Character development, while incredibly important to the evolution of your story, is one of the most rewarding parts of writing. You have the opportunity to create a hero, a villain, and a cast of supporting characters each with the chance to become a better – or worse – person. They can of course stay the same person, but everyone is enchanted by a character who reminds them of themselves even in some small way, and changes.

As writers, it is our responsibility to create believable characters. Everyone goes about this differently – and I invite you to pursue all of the subjects in this book more thoroughly – but my philosophy on the matter is made up of three parts:

1. Characters must be true to the world in which they are written
2. Characters must have a flaw
3. Characters must face a conflict and have the opportunity to make a change

I do not believe all characters have to be loved or liked, however you will have much better success if your main character is a person your readership likes to read about. So whether that means s/he is liked, respected, or simply empathized with, is up to you and your audience.

I personally feel my main character needs to be liked, have a flaw which readers can identify with, and my villain – while still a villain – is not *always* so horrible and bad, and sometimes has a flaw that readers can empathize or identify with. It makes for a more complex plot when rooting for the good guy isn't so black and white, and you have character development on both sides of the spectrum.

Character development can happen with all of your characters. It doesn't just need to happen with your protagonist (main good guy) and antagonist (main bad guy). In fact, I think it's important that it does – it provides more opportunity for conflict, tension, growth, and bonding.

The three points I addressed above have all been addressed briefly, but I will touch on them once again:

1. Characters must be true to the world in which they are written

    If your character suddenly starts talking like a scientist in the 1900's and he is a harpist in the 1800's, it's going to be very odd for the reader to believe in your character. It's important to be sure your character speaks, acts, and responds to his environment appropriately. Even if there is time-travel involved.

2. Characters must have a flaw

    As I've mentioned before, characters with flaws are believable and much more dynamic characters. Flaws give characters a chance to wonder or wish they were better at something or wish they didn't do something, and perhaps work throughout the story to improve on whatever that thing is. Or, to discover about themselves something we, as readers, already knew.

3. Characters must face a conflict and have the opportunity to make a change

Conflict is imperative because it's what the story is driving toward. It's what allows characters to change, or make life-changing decisions for themselves, or for the good – or ill – of many. This opportunity to face conflict is one both antagonists and protagonists should face. It tests our characters true nature and where any doubt readers may have about them, is laid to rest.

Character development is great fun and you, as a writer, can go anywhere with it. I've often thought of it as the chance to become a variety of characters I would never actually be, but could explore to the maximum. And the best part, I can always write my own endings – and rewrite them if they didn't work out the way I wanted.

Character Development Exercises

ONE

Write a list of all the characters in your story.

On a separate page for each character, write out a character sketch including:

- Name
- Physical description
- Likes, dislikes

- Age
- Family history
- Favorite activities

- Gender
- Physical location (past, present)
- Most memorable experience

TWO

Identify two – five of your main characters.

After you've done the above character sketch, identify the flaws for each of these characters.

Then, consider where you'd like these characters to be by the end of the story. They don't have to end up here since we know writing doesn't always end the way we think it will - but for now, jot something down.

If you can, write down a few events that may help them get to this point. If that's too much planning, that's okay! We don't all work with outlines.

Hang onto this – see where your characters end up at when your story is complete.

Worldbuilding

Worldbuilding is where you get to create the universe in which your characters live and breathe, and where your story takes place.

You've already discovered the basics of creating believable characters. You know how to write believable dialogue. And you know how to put it all together to bring your readers into your story by showing and not telling.

The worldbuilding process takes what we've covered so far and puts it into practice by applying it to the creation of the world your story takes place in.

This is a fun part of story creation. Like characters, you can create your world to be anything you want, and tweak it to suit your needs. However you do need to establish a consistent framework for your world and stick to it throughout.

When building your world, there are at least five aspects to consider and develop:

1. History

a) The timeline for your world. Go back as far as you like, but be sure you include recent history and how it influences your characters.

2. Geography

b) How the world's landscape effects the shape of the story, characters decisions, how it helps/hinders their progress, etc.

3. Zoology/Ecology

c) The wildlife or biology in the world. What wildlife or biology exist/existed in this world? How does it relate or interact with your characters and plot?

4. Sociology

d) Social behavior, organization, interactions. What social structure is there? How was it established and where do your characters fit? How does it affect their decisions or influence their role? What social restrictions are there?

5. Economy

   e) What sort of economic structure is your world set up as? Is there trade, does money pass hands, is it a feudal system, republic, something completely new? Is your character influenced by money? Where does he stand in the economic structure of your world?

Some writers love to develop each of these elements in their entirety and write entire histories, develop planetary systems, and create a complex economy. While that can never hurt, in fact it will add incredible depth to your story by showing intimate familiarity with your world, it isn't entirely necessary.

It is important to develop enough of each that it is clear you and your characters are comfortable and knowledgeable about the world. Not only that, but you need to know your world so well you don't accidentally write in an inconsistency somewhere. For example, you refer to the north as being hot and swampy, but later you refer to it being rugged and windy. Knowing your world through and through prevents that.

Worldbuilding Exercises

ONE

Describe your world in a few paragraphs or pages. Let your mind explore all options and try not to limit yourself to the normal, unless that's your intent.

Can you visualize your characters there? Can you see them interacting and moving easily throughout the world? Do you see yourself able to 'show don't tell' when you write about the world? Do you feel you know this world intimately?

TWO

Take each of the below elements and develop each of them to the best of your ability, or to where you feel you have a good grasp of your world:

1. History
2. Geography
3. Zoology/Ecology
4. Sociology

5. Economy

Here are two websites I'd like to refer you to for more exercises and information on worldbuilding. They are interesting, informative, and helpful. I hope you enjoy and are inspired!

http://www.web-writer.net/fantasy/days/ - 30 days of worldbuilding exercises (15 minutes/day)

http://worldbuildingschool.com/ - website dedicated to worldbuilding

Pacing

Have you ever read a book and wondered when they'd get to the point? Or when the action would start? Or have you been completely enthralled with the story line only to have it come to a screeching halt by going off in an entirely different direction for pages?

This has to do with a story's pacing.

Pacing deals both with the story's timeframe and how fast or slow we as readers perceive the story is moving.

As readers, we need the right mix of dialogue, narrative, and action for the particular genre we are reading. It takes practice, but you'll develop your own sense of pacing appropriate for your style of writing.

Dialogue can carry action, as can narrative, so there are many ways to move the story forward without boring the reader or diverting to tangents. As a general rule, if your pages are full of dialogue only, your readers won't get a good sense of environment or anything else happening around the character unless you make excellent use of tags.

But, as we mentioned earlier, overuse of tags can be annoying.

How to remedy that? By mixing dialogue with narrative so the reader has the sense they are listening in on the conversation from a park bench, or the next coffee table – somewhere in the same environment where they pick up sensory imagery and overall shared moods of the characters, while still listening in on the conversation.

Another trick that will help readers continue with your story is sentence structure. Long drawn out sentences take much longer to read and people can get lost in them. Alternating medium, short, and long sentences can help the story's pacing and flow.

If you have multiple long sentences in one paragraph, one after the other, the reader might get the impression the character is being reflective. On the other hand, if there are a handful of short sentences all in a row, the reader might feel tension or that the character is anxious, gearing up for some action. Sentence structure sends subliminal messages to our brains as we read. Again, read your paragraphs aloud and you'll hear it.

The story isn't a race, but you have an obligation to your readers to keep them hooked. They just paid for *your* book, make sure they can't put it down.

A great way to do this by creating chapters that end on a cliff-hanger. If you have developed a character people are drawn to, then put them in situations where if they simply 'turn the page, they'll find out what happens next…' they'll do that until the end and they'll want to go out and buy the next book.

One of my favorite examples of this is the Jack Reacher series by Lee Child. They're like Pringles: once you pop, you can't stop!

Your timeline doesn't even have to be long – the entire book could be one day or a couple days. What matters is setting up your scenes where the events, the pacing, happens in a realistic way – but honing in on the good parts.

If there is a crime scene, your readers won't want to read descriptions of how the paramedics arrived, got out of their vehicles, unloaded their equipment, then they went to work and a crowd gathered etc.,….what they'll want to know is the nitty gritty details of your characters thoughts as the detective, what clues she's found, why she keyed in on one of the observers in the crowed, what the results were of the autopsy, etc. All that other stuff is background noise. You can mention it, but in a carefully crafted line or two so it delivers the most imagery in the least space.

When you write, you want to share with your readers the best parts of all the scenes you are imagining and the juiciest parts of all the conversations you are hearing. Then, leave them with an irresistible question, comment, dilemma, observation, etc. and they can't help but find out what's on the opposite side of the page. That is what will keep them reading.

Pacing Exercises

ONE

Read your story aloud and see if there are any areas where you have sentences of similar length bunched together. If so, see how you can break them apart by rewriting, combining, or moving them around.

TWO

As you read through your story, see if there are areas with too much unnecessary narrative. If you are having trouble spotting it, print your story (or a portion of it) out and lay it page by page on the table/ground.

If you find large sections of block text with few lines of dialogue, those might be areas to target.

See diagram on the next page.

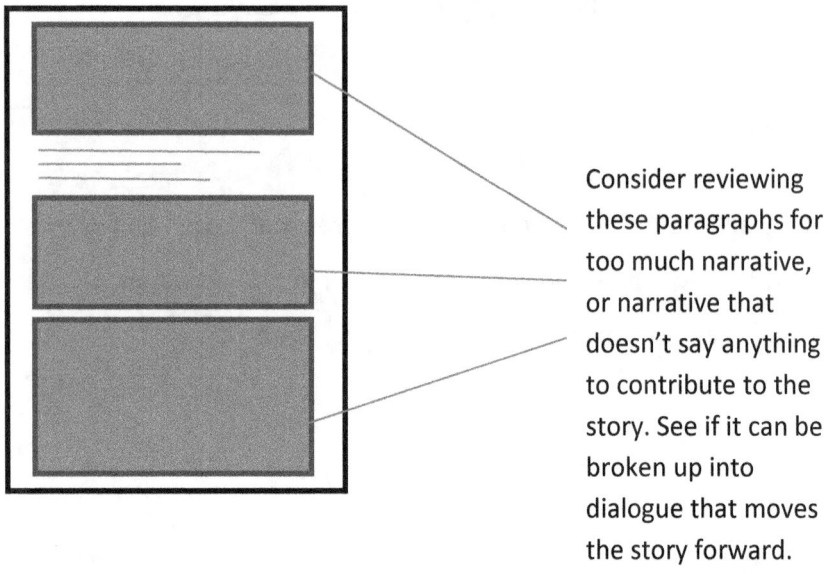

Consider reviewing these paragraphs for too much narrative, or narrative that doesn't say anything to contribute to the story. See if it can be broken up into dialogue that moves the story forward.

THREE

Rewrite sections of your text with what we discussed above in mind. See if you find any changes you like!

Fact Consistency

We've covered this in some detail already. It's unavoidable.

When you write, you want to be sure everything in your story remains constant and true to what was said throughout.

So be sure that Sue Samson at the beginning of the novel doesn't accidentally become Sam Susan at the end. Confirm that your promise 'boy vows to meet girl and marry her' at the beginning of the story actually happens, or if it doesn't, the evolution of that change is demonstrated clearly throughout the story and has a resolution at the end.

And of course be sure that if you are quoting or referring to actual facts (people, history, books, etc), that you spell them, refer to their date, quote them correctly. It lessens your credibility to say, 'My favorite author is Edgar Alan Po' when it's spelled Edgar Allan Poe.

It is surprising how unforgiving readers are in this department. Please be sure you triple check all your facts –

even if they are new, made-up facts applicable only to your newly formed world. There are readers out there who will check you on it and hold you accountable.

Fact Consistency Exercise

ONE

As you create your world and new characters, keep a list.

Find a method that works for you so you can keep track of what you've created, what attributes they have, and how they've evolved throughout the story.

Methods could include:

- A spreadsheet
- A physical map – as in the case of a world landscape
- Mind mapping
- A white board
- Using a computer program such as WriteItNow or WriteWay Pro

Meet the Author

I'm Joy Burke. I'm a freelance writer and developmental editor in Washington state and author of *A Book of Shorts: Stories from Various Drawers*. Creative writing has been my first love for over 25 years. I have been a freelance professional business writer since 2012 with clients including Gilpin Real Estate, King Enterprises, and Everett Chiropractic Center. As I transition into Northwest Women Writers Coordinator, I have also shifted my focus to helping aspiring writers reach their full potential by bringing Haha! Ink! Creative Studios front and center.

I look forward to working with authors from all walks of life and at every stage of the journey.

Here's to your success and creativity!

Let's Connect

I hope you've enjoyed *Fundamentals of Creative Writing* and have found some useful tidbits you can start applying right away.

If you are interested in learning more, have questions, or have a manuscript you'd like to work on, please let me know. I'd love to work with you!

You can find me online at:

Website: www.hahaink.com

Twitter: @joyaburke

LinkedIn: linkedin.com/in/joyaburke

Email: contact@hahaink.com

Happy Writing!

Also By Joy...

A Book of Shorts:
Stories from Various Drawers

Creating Memorable & Dynamic Characters:
Creating Personalities Readers Will Identify with and Believe In

Picking Up:
A Book of Story Starts

Coming Soon!

The GREAT^{SM} Principle
Content Marketing made Easy